Bare, Beautiful Feet

and Other Missionary Stories for Children

Compiled from past issues of *The Alliance World* (a missionary education tool published by Christian Publications)

Illustrated by Elynne Chudnovsky

CHRISTIAN PUBLICATIONS / Camp Hill, Pennsylvania

D1607051

The mark of vibrant faith

Christian Publications
3825 Hartzdale Drive, Camp Hill, PA 17011

© 1992 by Christian Publications. All rights
reserved.
ISBN: 0-87509-485-6
LOC Catalog Card Number: 91-78296
Printed in the United States of America

92 93 94 95 96   5 4 3 2 1

Scripture quotations are from the HOLY
BIBLE: NEW INTERNATIONAL VER-
SION. Copyright © 1973, 1978, 1984 by the
International Bible Society. Used by permis-
sion of Zondervan Bible Publishers.

Contents

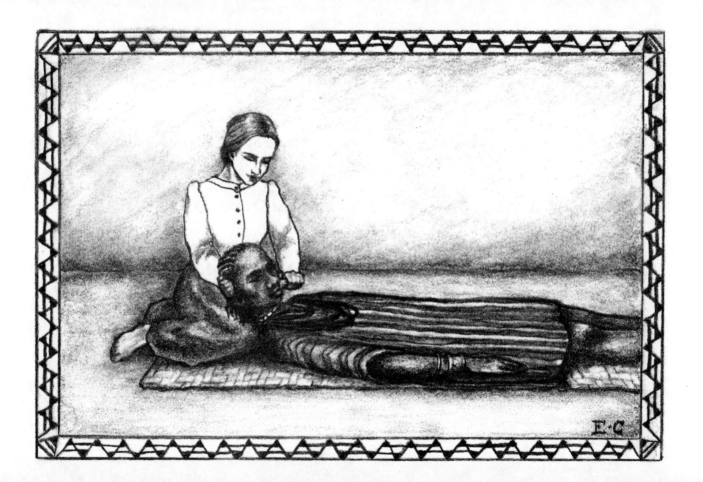

Bare, Beautiful Feet

This is the true story of Mary Slessor (1848–1915). As a child, Mary was so timid that she was afraid to walk across a field with a cow in it. But when she heard about the warriors in Africa who would kill 20 people in a raid, she offered to go as a missionary. God used Mary Slessor for many years in Africa. This is just one of the exciting stories of her life.

It was very quiet in the village by the river—very quiet indeed. The people were waiting for death. Their chief lay in his hut so sick they knew he would die, and if he died it meant many of them would die, too. That was the custom. Some of his wives, soldiers and slaves would be killed to go with him into the spirit world. Can't you hear their hearts beating in fear in the eerie silence?

As they waited, trembling, a woman from another African village appeared. She told them, "There lives away through the forest at Ekenge a white *Ma* who can cast out by her magic the demons who are killing your chief. Let your chief send for her and he will not die." *Ma* was a term of respect. Word was sent to the dying chief and he commanded that this person be sent for.

It took eight hours for the messengers to reach Ekenge where Mary Slessor lived. When she heard the request she said, "I must go to him." She knew she might be killed by enemy warriors or wild beasts. She knew the streams were deep and that rain could come, but she insisted, "I must go."

The chief of Mary's village provided women to go along to care for her and men to protect her. It was already raining when they left her village. It was coming down in sheets—pouring and pouring and pouring. Mary Slessor's boots got so soaked she couldn't walk in them, so she took them off and threw them into the bushes. Soon her stock-ings followed and on and on she plowed in the mud—bare, beautiful feet! For more than eight hours Mary Slessor walked, almost without stopping.

Though the weather cleared, her head throbbed with fever. Aching from head to foot with fever and tiredness, she reached the sick chief's village. She didn't lie down for even a moment's rest but went directly to his hut. He lay unconscious on his mat on the mud floor.

Mary Slessor examined the chief, took a drug from her little medicine chest and gave some to the dying man. But she knew at once that he needed more of the medicine that she had with her. She knew of another missionary several hours away and told the people they would have to go there for more medicine. They were afraid and would not go because it was enemy territory and they could be killed. But someone remembered there was a man from that country living in his canoe on the river. Would he go? Someone ran to the river to ask him. At first he refused, but finally he agreed. The next day he returned with the medicine.

Gradually, the chief they had thought was almost dead regained consciousness. One day he sat up and ate food, and at last he was well again. The whole village rejoiced! They could live! No wives or soldiers or slaves needed to be killed!

The people wondered at Mary Slessor's "magic" powers. But she told them she had come because she worshiped the true God who had made their great forest. And she told them about the Great Physician, Jesus Christ. She gathered them together morning and evening and led them as they all thanked God for healing their chief.

Mary Slessor was a missionary pioneer who lived in the 1800s. Some day when we all get to heaven we will be able to meet this woman whom God says has beautiful feet. Do only missionaries have beautiful feet? No, anyone who tells others of Christ's love is helping to spread the good news.

The Missing Wallet

He thought he would never get it back! He was angry! Why didn't God show him where it was? What good would it do anyone else?

For seven years Doug had been making a valuable collection—piece by piece, here a little, there a little, and now the whole bunch was gone! And it was all for God's work, too! Didn't God care? Doug was doubting God.

What was in this collection that was so valuable to Doug? For seven years he had been working in Santiago, Chile, as a missionary. Whenever he would meet a person who he thought might be interested in hearing more about Jesus or who had a part in ministering the gospel with him, Doug would jot down his or her name, address and phone number in his little book. He had made so many contacts, and all the names and numbers were together. He just couldn't replace such a collection.

Doug and his wife, Ann, had been out visiting for the Lord that Wednesday night. They had talked to someone who was unsaved and had opened her heart to the Lord. It made them happy to know that God was using them in Chile and that another person had come to know Jesus. I'm sure that name went down in Doug's little book that evening. When they got home around midnight they were content because they knew their evening had been spent well. They were also very tired so they went right to bed.

It was still pitch black out when they heard a noise. They thought the puppy wanted to be let out. Ann went to the puppy but as she was letting it out, she kept hearing noises. She realized that it wasn't the dog that was making them! *Well, maybe it's Brandon,* she thought,

so she called out his name. But it wasn't her son! Suddenly she heard the set of bells on the front door ringing. She yelled out, "Doug, someone just went out the front door!"

Doug was on his feet and running. There wasn't time to get dressed and so in shorts and socks he got out the car and began to search the streets around their house. He found nothing.

In a few minutes, Brandon came out and took over the car search while Doug put on some clothes and began a search on foot. On the sidewalk just a bit up the street from the house, he found his leather jacket. *Aha,* he thought, *I'm on the right track.*

Near the house is a hill covered with small bushes and briars. As Doug stood at the bottom of the hill, he could hear someone moving. *Do I go in after him?* he wondered.

It was still completely dark and he was nervous about going in, but Doug decided to risk it. It was so dark he could barely see where he was going. After a few minutes, Doug saw someone crouching down just ahead of him, trying to hide. He went closer. It was a young man.

"What are you doing here?" Doug asked.

"I'm on my way to work," was the answer. Doug knew he was lying. By now it was 4:30 a.m. and this man was hiding on the side of a hill that led to nowhere. Although Doug didn't believe the man, he acted as if he did. He told him a robbery had been committed within sight of where this man was. "Did you see anything?" Doug asked.

"No," was the reply. "I didn't see anything."

"Do you have any identification?" Doug asked.

"None," the man answered.

During the conversation it didn't occur to Doug that he might have been in danger. When Doug had first seen the man crouching down, he noticed that the man appeared to be hiding something under his poncho. Doug thought it might be one of their stolen things, so he asked, "What do you have hidden there?"

"It is my weapon," the man replied.

At this point Doug was more angry than afraid so he told him in a very commanding voice to stand up. To Doug's surprise the man obeyed him and even put both hands up in the air.

By now the police had arrived. Doug shouted out in English to his family to let them know where he was. The man with his hands up didn't know English, so he didn't realize that Doug was telling the police where he was. Soon the police took the man into custody.

While he was explaining to the police what happened, Doug led them to where he had found his jacket. When they got there Doug found his credit card, which had been in his wallet in the jacket. But no wallet was seen. They began to look in the bushes next to the sidewalk. Ann discovered a bag full of clothes. Soon they found the television set and the shortwave radio.

It wasn't light yet, so they went back to their house for a cup of coffee and to settle their nerves before the sun came up. At sunrise, Brandon and Doug went back to search for some other items still missing. It wasn't long before they found some more things, including two

10-speed bikes that had been stolen apparently to get away on. The only thing that they couldn't find was Doug's wallet. In his wallet was that important address book, quite a bit of cash and his important documents.

The next day Doug went to the police station to see if there was any news of his missing papers. They hadn't heard anything, but Doug did find out that they had arrested two other robbers who had been involved. The paper reported later that day that the gang had been robbing the neighborhood for some time. Doug became a hero on his block. Because of this he had two chances to talk about the Lord to people whom he hadn't met before.

Ten days went by. Doug was missing appointments because he didn't have his date book. He and Ann wondered if they were going to make ends meet financially because of losing their money. And then there was all the red tape of applying for a new license and a new identification card. Doug had felt that surely the Lord would let him get his date book and wallet back, but his faith was getting weaker.

On the 10th day, at 6:15 p.m., God sent two "angels" to their house.

"Sir, does this belong to you?" they asked.

Doug couldn't believe his eyes. There

in the man's hand was his wallet! God had been faithful. He had not let Doug down. Doug had doubted and been angry, but God remained faithful. Doug took the wallet in his hands. All of his contacts from seven years of work! Numbers and names that he couldn't replace! He opened the wallet and could hardly believe his eyes. All his papers were there! By now he was trembling. He opened the cash section and there was the money they so badly needed. The billfold had lain in the leaves and rubble along the sidewalk about two blocks from their house for 10 days! God had indeed sent two angels to return it. For the very first time since the robbery it rained that night. God's timing was perfect. He knew where that billfold was all that time and took good care of it. Doug was ashamed of his lack of faith and anger at God.

Modern Pilgrims

People have often come to North America to escape. Sometimes they were escaping religious persecution, like the Pilgrims. Others came to get away from racial discrimination, like the Jews. And still others came to look for a better life and to escape poverty. Even today people are anxious to escape and get to our free country—they are modern pilgrims.

KunBum Chheng is an example of a modern day pilgrim. She is a Cambodian who came to the U.S. When KunBum lived in Cambodia, she had seven children and five grandsons. Her husband was a captain in the army. When the communist Khmer Rouge took over, her family was separated. Some died and some were lost. Her husband was taken away by the commander of the Khmer Rouge in 1975. In 1979 one of her sons, one of her daughters and KunBum escaped from Cambodia to a refugee camp in Thailand. Another daughter and her family escaped later. In all only three children and one grandson were left alive.

KunBum lived in a refugee camp named K.D. One day she was sitting in front of her hut, and she saw her son coming toward her. He said, "Today I met one of my old friends on the street. He is a Christian. He wants me to study the Bible with him. Do you care if I study with him?" Her son gave her a small piece of paper that told about Jesus Christ. When she read it, she became very happy. She was interested in what this friend could teach her son, so she let him go to church.

When her son came back from church, she saw a new Bible in his hand. She took it from him and read it all day. She didn't understand it, and so she asked her son if the church let old people study there. He answered yes.

At that time her son and she smoked cigarettes. She would often buy cigarettes at the small store on the west side of the camp. One day KunBum walked the wrong way to the store—she didn't know why. But then she found the church. She had never seen it before. She saw a crowd of people and heard them singing, so she stopped and listened.

Soon a woman carrying books came along. She was giving books to everyone around her, but she didn't share one with KunBum. KunBum asked for one of the books. The woman said, "Do you believe in God? Why do you want one of the books?"

Just to get a book, KunBum replied, "Yes, I believe and I want to have one of the books." So the woman gave her one.

KunBum went home and read the book to the end, but she still didn't understand it. She decided to study the Bible and to offer herself to God.

She began to learn how to pray. She and her son praised God and asked Him to wash the sin from their family. They asked Him to help them quit smoking cigarettes. They prayed for God's help and soon they no longer smoked.

KunBum's knees were very painful and she could not walk well. She prayed to God to heal her painful knees. They grew worse. She would groan at night in her sleep because of the pain. Her son heard her and said, "If you trust God, believe in Him and pray to Him every day and night, you will get well."

Her son's words opened her heart to believe and trust God. She asked her son to pray with her that night. They prayed together until midnight and then went to sleep.

The next morning when she rose from her bamboo bed, the pain was gone from KunBum's knees. She moved her legs around and her knees no longer hurt. She was very happy and walked around the camp sharing her testimony.

Many friends believed, and about 20 people went to church with her. At night she invited them to her home to sing praises to God, read the Bible and pray together. She did this until her family moved to another refugee camp called Kamp Put. Later, KunBum came to the United States. Now she does not have to go from one refugee camp to another. She attends a Cambodian church and hears God's Word preached. The church KunBum attends is one of many churches in North America for people who leave their own countries and come here for different reasons.

The Raft Ride

Esther was excited. She and Becky and Lucing were going to hike into the mountains. They were going to visit three little mountain churches among the Subanen people to hold Sunday school conventions. On their return trip, they would get to ride a raft down the river. That sounded like fun!

It took about five hours to reach the first little church. They hiked over rough trails and crossed the river five times by foot. There were no bridges over the river, but that was OK with Esther because she loved the water and the challenge. All the baggage was carried by young boys, so that Esther and her friends could walk easier.

Finally they reached the top of the mountain where the first small church was located. The poor people of the village had no pastor, but they had built a parsonage anyway. They hoped and prayed that the Lord would soon send them someone to preach to them.

The village people fixed some rice and pork for the women's supper, and after that, it was time for bed. Esther, Becky, and Lucing slept on a mat under one big mosquito net which just barely fit in the room. It was so good to stretch out on the bamboo floor and rest their tired legs. The first day's hike was over and all was well.

That night, Esther woke up sick. As she lay in misery on the mat, she didn't know what she was going to do. The others would have to teach the classes without her. But what about the trip to the next church? Would she be able to make it?

When the others thought she was asleep, she heard them talking in another room: "Well, I don't know what we'll do. She's too sick to hike. I suppose we could get a carabao (cah-rah-bah-oh) and take her out." Carabaos are the work animals of the Philippines—in some countries they are called water buffaloes. Carabaos are strong and pull bamboo sleds which the Filipinos make.

As she lay there, Esther remembered a part of God's Word she had read recently. The Israelites were marching against their enemy and the Lord told them to have the singers go *before* the army *praising* the Lord (2 Chronicles 20:21–22). When they did that, the Lord gave them a great victory.

Well, this sickness was really an "enemy" on this trip, and Esther decided she would do what the Lord told the Israelites to do—she began to *praise* the Lord. When they got up the next day, all three ladies started down the mountain trail. As she went, Esther was singing, "They shall run and not be weary, they shall walk and not faint."

The hike was longer that day—nine hours—and harder. But Esther walked on and on. The farther she walked, the better she felt. The Lord had healed her!

The three ladies visited the other two churches on their schedule and held the classes. When all the work was finished, the women hiked down to the river for the big raft ride home. How glad Esther was that she didn't have to miss it.

Becky and Lucing were not quite as excited about the trip as Esther was, though. They didn't much like the water because they couldn't swim. There were three rafts ready for them. The baggage was tied onto one raft, Becky and Lucing sat on another, and Esther took the lead raft. A man stood on each raft to steer with a long pole.

Esther kept watch on the other rafts as they made their way down the river. As she glanced back one time, she saw the second raft hit a high bank and turn on its side. Becky and Lucing were knocked off, but they were able to scramble ashore. That took some fast moving! After the raft had been righted, the party continued on.

Esther kept checking on them, even though she wasn't really close enough to help. On one of those backward glances, however, the raft behind her was very near and the pole man brought down his long stick—right on Esther's nose! Ouch! Still, she thoroughly enjoyed the ride on the river and was thankful that she could come out of the mountains by raft and not by carabao sled.

A Different Kind of Hunt

Many years ago, Zaire was called Congo. The mighty river running through the country was also called the Congo. George Grenfell, a young man from England, hunted along the river. He had a boat built in England. It was taken apart, and the pieces were packed in 800 boxes weighing 65 pounds each. The boxes were shipped to the mouth of the river, where 1,000 men picked up the bundles and carried them miles through the jungle. When they got past the rapids on the river, the boat was reassembled. George Grenfell used the boat, named *Peace*, on his hunting expeditions. What was he hunting for? For people who needed to hear the gospel!

One day George paddled ashore to a village where he found two young girls tied to a stake. He learned from the chief that the tribe had gone up the river, raided another village and captured the girls. Now they were selling them as slaves. That was a horrible kind of hunting, wasn't it?

George Grenfell didn't want slaves, but he couldn't stand seeing the girls suf-

fer so he bought them from the chief. They must have wondered what the strange man was going to do with them as they jumped into his canoe and went out to the *Peace*. They had never seen a big boat before. It looked like a huge river monster to them.

As the *Peace* made its way upriver, it rounded a bend and another village came into view. On the bank of the river warriors stood holding spears. In the water were canoes with warriors also armed with spears. A few weeks before, enemies had come up the river and raided the village. Now the *Peace* had come from the same direction. At a signal from the chief, the warriors began hurling their lances at the boat. The spears glanced off the steel screen surrounding the deck where Grenfell stood with the two girls. Suddenly one of the girls shouted and waved her arms.

"What is it?" Grenfell asked.

The girl pointed at one of the warriors. "That is my brother! This is my village!"

Grenfell told her to call to her brother, but the warriors were making so much noise that the girl couldn't be heard. Then Grenfell gave an order to the pilot and a piercing shriek sounded on the river—the boat's whistle. The warriors had never heard a steamer's whistle before and were instantly quiet.

Grenfell whispered to the girl, "Call again," and she did. That surprised the warrior. He began paddling swiftly to the *Peace* and soon met his lost sister. He also heard how the man in "the canoe that smoked" had saved her from slavery.

The girls were delighted to be home, and the warriors put away their weapons. I think George Grenfell found those people willing to listen to the gospel, don't you?

George Grenfell's hunt for souls ended in 1906. His was the best kind of hunt. But that was long ago. Are people still hunting in Zaire? You bet they are! And I'm glad to tell you the terrible hunts for slaves no longer happen, but the best kind of hunting is still going on.

In Zaire, the people like to tell stories, some of which are fables—that is, they are stories with a lesson hidden in them. Here is a fable Zairians tell about hunting.

A man purchased a gun. He knew it was good and accurate, so he got in his canoe and crossed the river to hunt on the other side. He was successful, killing a large antelope. He carried the animal back to the river, but when he got to the bank his canoe was gone—it had been carried away by the current. So the hunter waited until a fisherman came along. The fisherman agreed to carry the man across the river, but the canoe was too small for the antelope. So the hunter refused to go. Later in the evening another fisherman came along and offered the hunter a ride. But the man in the boat would not carry the antelope. The hunter decided to camp out until morning. He cut some meat and put it over a fire. But while he waited for the meat to cook, a lion came and killed him.

The antelope in this fable could stand for sin in a person's life. Some lost people are not willing to leave their sin and come to Jesus for salvation.

There is a group in Zaire called the Bateke tribe. These people speak a different language from the Zairians with whom the missionaries were working. No one had gone to tell the Bateke about Jesus because the Bateke live in a place where there are not many roads. Missionaries need a four-wheel drive truck to get into many of the villages.

The Alliance Church and mission in Zaire decided to go hunting in this difficult area. So far, four North American missionaries have gone along with a Zairian pastor and a national doctor.

Many of the Bateke people practice witchcraft, so we need to pray that they will not be like the man in the fable. Satan will not want them to give up their evil worship to follow Christ. He will fight hard to keep these people from becoming Christians. But the Bible says no one can serve two masters. The Bateke will have to give up their witchcraft to become God's children.

People who hunt need weapons. The slave hunters used guns to force people to obey them. The man in the fable used a gun to kill the antelope. But what weapon did George Grenfell have? What about our missionaries today? The Bible and prayer!

Kept Safe by the Love of Jesus

It would be terrible if no one wanted you, wouldn't it? A little girl named Marta lived in the country of Ecuador, South America. Marta's mother and father were divorced, and she lived with her mother, who did not really want her. She beat her and did not give her enough to eat.

In the town where little Marta lived, a missionary family started some children's Bible classes. A neighbor invited Marta to come.

"Did you notice how thin and ragged that poor little girl is?" the missionary lady asked her husband.

"Yes."

"She has big bruises and welts where someone hits her. I hope she comes back to Bible classes," she said.

Marta did come back every week.

One day the missionaries invited her to come home with them for supper. Never in her life had she seen so much food. And she was told to eat *all* that she wanted.

It was not long before Marta spent more time at the home of the mission-

ary couple than she did at her own house. They began to invite her to spend the night, and sometimes she stayed with them for one or two weeks.

At the missionaries' house, Marta ate good food. She took baths and scrubbed herself clean. Her new friends bought her clothes that fit her. She felt *so* happy.

Sometimes her mother demanded that she come home. And every time she returned to her own house, it was not long before she was hungry and dirty and sad all over again.

"I would like to adopt Marta," the missionary lady said.

Her husband agreed and replied, "Let's talk to her mother."

Marta's mother consented. After much paperwork, Marta had a new family! This time, she had a family that loved and wanted her. She loved her new family, too. She also loved going to church with her new parents.

Marta listened to all the Bible stories over and over. She sang children's choruses. She won sticks of candy for memorizing Bible verses. One of the verses Marta memorized was Matthew 19:14. Her new family often told her how much Jesus loved her.

"How could He love me when my own mother didn't?"

"You are a special little girl," they told her.

"Sometimes people don't love us as they should, but Jesus always does." Marta started to believe she was loved.

"I have a new verse for you to memorize," the Bible class teacher told the children one day.

"For God so loved the world . . ." Marta mumbled the verse over and over to herself. Everywhere she went she practiced the verse.

"All right, now who can say our Bible verse for us?" the teacher asked during the next class. Marta's hand shot up.

"Go ahead, Marta," said the teacher. Marta started to say the verse and stopped.

"What is wrong?" asked the teacher.

"Jesus died for me!" Marta's face grew red and tears filled her huge brown eyes. "I just now understood that He *does* love me!"

That day, Marta asked Jesus to come into her heart. She memorized more Bible verses than ever now that she knew Jesus as her own personal Savior. In Sunday school, she learned enough verses to win a New Testament. She hugged her Bible to her and promised herself that she would carry it with her wherever she went.

One day Marta skipped along the street toward home with her New Testament tucked under her arm. All of a sudden someone grabbed her from behind.

"Help! Help!" she tried to scream, but a hand clamped tightly over her mouth. Dragging her to a waiting car, the kidnapper threw her into the back seat and sped off.

Marta's new family waited for her to come home. Night came and still she did not return. They finally went to the neighbors.

"Have you seen Marta?" they asked. Everyone helped them look, but Marta had disappeared. No one knew where she had gone.

The day came when Marta's missionary family had to leave Ecuador. Their hearts were broken. They knew that somewhere Marta needed them.

Years passed and people forgot about Marta. But the missionary family never did. No matter where they went, they prayed for her each day, and in their hearts, they still loved her.

Back in Ecuador, a young man named Adan asked Jesus to come into his heart. One day, in the little church where Adan worshipped, he noticed a beautiful young lady.

"Hello," he said, "my name is Adan. Welcome."

"My name is Marta," the young lady told him.

Marta and Adan fell in love, and soon they were married. Adan was shocked when she told him about her past.

She was 12 years old when the kidnapper snatched her off the street, and for months afterward, she had been locked inside a tiny, dingy room. It was her very own mother who had kidnapped her!

"She beat me with shoes or plates or whatever she could find. But I never forgot the Bible verses I had memorized. They helped me to go on living. And I hid my precious New Testament where Mother couldn't see it, so I could read the words of my Jesus," Marta cried as she related the story of her past to Adan.

"Let's try to find your missionary family," Adan suggested. It took time, but they finally found Marta's family.

Can you guess what happened when they met again? They hugged, laughed and cried, all at the same time.

"There is one special Bible verse that I kept in my heart through everything," Marta told her family. "Whenever things got so bad that I thought I wouldn't make it, Deuteronomy 31:6 kept me going."

Jesus never left Marta during all those years when she was being hurt. He loved her and cared about her.

The Best Friend

The Sunday school children were having a hard time keeping still. Today they were having a special visitor, and every boy and girl knew that when Rev. Ho came, it was a special time. They stood around in groups laughing and chatting and telling each other how glad they were that the special guest was coming. But there was one boy who stood off all by himself. He was a quiet boy and didn't say much, and the other children mostly left him to himself.

Finally the moment arrived, and the guest came up the walk toward the church. With smiles and nods he greeted the children and made them feel that he thought they were the nicest children in the whole world. Then suddenly he stopped, right where the quiet boy stood. He looked down at him and said, "I don't believe I know you. What is your name?"

"David," the boy replied, hanging his head.

"Well, isn't that remarkable! I am a David, too. Why are you standing here all by yourself?"

"I'm new here. My parents brought me here a couple of Sundays ago and

told me I have to come every Sunday, and I don't know anybody."

"I know just how you feel. Let's sit down here on this step. I want to tell you about another boy who thought he was the loneliest boy in the world."

Quietly the children gathered around Rev. Ho and David as they settled themselves on the step.

"David, by the time the boy in our story was as old as you, he had been in five different schools. Every time the family moved and he had to start in a new school, he hated it. He hated being laughed at for mistakes he made. It seemed that he never stayed anywhere long enough to feel comfortable.

"Then one day something happened that made the boy feel much better. A man and a woman visited his home and invited the family to their church. The boy's father was not interested, but the boy asked if he might go and take his younger brothers and sister with him. The very next Sunday morning, with their father's permission, the little group went off to their first day in Sunday school. There the boy in our story was taken into a class where he met Mrs. Birkey. She had such a kind face and such a warm smile that he began to feel that he might be happy in her class. And he was. She made him feel so welcome. And she made all the children feel as if she really and truly loved them—and I am sure she did.

"It was in that Sunday school that the boy learned about a friend who would be with us wherever we go—one who would never leave us and who would never laugh at the dumb things we do sometimes. Do you know who that friend is?"

"I didn't know there was such a friend," answered David. "I wish I could find a friend like that. I don't have any brothers or sisters or friends or anybody."

"Well, David," said Rev. Ho, "that friend is Jesus, God's Son. And that little boy heard that if he invited Jesus to come and be his friend, he would never ever have to be lonely. And the boy bowed his head and told Jesus he wanted Him to be his friend. And that friend never left him, even when he had hard things to do.

"Our story boy kept moving with his family, and then it was time to enter high school." Rev. Ho looked around the group and said, "I am sure your older brothers and sisters and friends have all told you about how hard that is. Every teenager is scared that he or she might not pass and then not be able to find any jobs except to clean streets or carry heavy loads where men are putting up high buildings. The boy was worried because he had changed schools so many times, but he prayed and studied hard, and his friend, Jesus, helped him to pass the tests.

"Later the boy learned to play the guitar, and when his family moved to Taipei, he went to a church where he was able to lead the singing.

"And then the boy was a young man, and it was time for him to enter the army. That really scared him. But again his friend was with him every day for two whole years. Even though the enemies of his country shot at him and the other soldiers with big cannons, and even though sometimes the shells came close to where he was, the young man was not afraid. His friend, Jesus, was right beside him.

"After the young man in our story got out of the army, he wanted to serve Jesus and tell others about Him. When he told his father, his father was not pleased. He said that if the son would forget this foolish notion and stay at home, he would give him enough money to own his own business. The young man wondered if this is what his friend Jesus would want him to do. After he prayed, he was sure that he wanted to preach about Jesus. So he packed his clothing and went off to Bible school. His parents would not give him any money, but kind Christian people were anxious for him to work for the Lord, and they helped him get through school.

"Later that young man got married and had a family. Even when he became a preacher, he still counted on Jesus' help.

"Once while a church service was going on, his little girl fell out of an upstairs window. The young man rushed out of the church to find his daughter lying unconscious on the sidewalk. While he took her by taxi to the nearest doctor's office, the people in the church prayed. Their prayers were answered. She did not even have one broken bone.

"This Jesus has done so many wonderful things for that young man that he can hardly believe it. And guess what? His father has come to believe in Jesus, too.

"David, would you like to invite Jesus into your life right now, to be *your* special friend?" asked Rev. Ho.

"Oh, yes," responded David. And together they prayed. After the prayer was over, David looked up with a great big wide smile on his face. The children began to smile back at him as though they wanted to know him better and be his friend.

"And now, my little friends," said Rev. Ho, becoming quite solemn. "Do you know what Jesus likes to have us do when someone new comes into our Sunday school?"

The children hung their heads for a moment and then said, "Rev. Ho, we're sorry. We should have been nicer to David. We want to tell Jesus we're sorry and that we will all be kinder to others."

After Rev. Ho had prayed with them, they all asked, "Tell us, Rev. Ho, you were the boy in the story, weren't you?" Rev. Ho just smiled and said, "Guess," and walked into the church.

The Meaning of the Cross

Fani sat in her bedroom not knowing what to do. She thought of her mother. Sometimes she wouldn't see her for three months. She remembered other times when she and her sister, Vicki, would hear her mother fighting with a bad man she was living with. Life was so mixed up and unhappy.

Today Fani was bored as she absentmindedly walked over and opened the closet door. Looking in she saw a Bible that she had been given by the Jehovah's Witnesses. For some reason she didn't understand, she felt like reading it, and she asked Vicki if it was OK to read it to her. When she finished, Fani said, "That was beautiful!" and she began reading the Bible every day.

But one day she read something about blood that seemed strange to her. She wanted to be sure she had the *true* Bible like the one she saw someone else using. Her mother agreed to buy her one. Fani was so excited when they went shopping. When they found a Bible, Fani asked the salesgirl, "Is this the *true* Bible or is there one even more authentic?"

The salesgirl answered, "Yes, yes, this is the Bible. There isn't any other."

Fani carried her Bible clutched to her side as they went home. She didn't want anyone else to touch it. It was a great treasure to her, and she could hardly wait to read it. Almost every night Fani read her new Bible.

It was only 12 days until her birthday and Fani wanted her mother to buy her something else—a gold cross. She didn't understand the meaning of the cross, but she was anxious to have one to wear. Often she had asked Vicki, who was three years younger, "What is so significant about the cross? Why is it so important?"

Vicki would reply, "Fani, Christians wear a cross because Jesus died on the cross."

But Fani kept feeling there was something she didn't understand. Even so, she could hardly wait until her birthday when she would get her gold cross.

The desire to read the Bible and to know the significance of the cross—and even to own a cross—was a mystery to her. Why did she want these things? She didn't know where the desire came from, but it was there—strange and strong!

In those days Fani wasn't a Christian. She didn't know what she wanted and her life revolved around going to parties with her friends. There she found different kinds of people doing many wrong things. She watched them and thought, "What would happen if I did these wrong things, too? Mother wouldn't care a bit. She is living with a man who is neither her husband nor my father. And what about life? It really isn't all that bad to do what you feel like doing, is it?"

When Fani finished eighth grade she quit school. She was confused and didn't know what to do with her life. She would ask herself, "Should I take drugs like my friends? Maybe that way I could find something worth living for." But even though she thought about taking drugs and doing other wrong things, there was something that kept her from doing them.

Fani continued to read her new Bible, but again she found something about blood that confused her. Did she really have the *true* Bible? She began to have nightmares about having to read the Bible. She was afraid that if she didn't, something bad would happen to her. When she woke up in the morning, she was full of fear. Why were these things happening to her?

One day when Fani and her sister were visiting in the home of a friend, their friend's mother began to talk to them about the Bible. Fani's comment was, "Did you know that the Bible isn't true?" The woman said it was and tried to encourage them to read the gospels. She also told them where an evangelical church was located.

Fani's birthday came on August 25, and she received the gold cross she had wanted so badly. She still didn't understand about the cross, but she was happy to have it.

She had been excited to hear about the evangelical church, so as soon as she could, she went to a service. There she asked many questions. She liked what she heard, and she particularly liked the youth group. Soon she became a regular attender at the youth meetings, outings and other services. Her mother told her not to go to church, but Fani kept going anyway.

Of course Fani had been wearing her birthday present, but the meaning of the cross was still not clear to her. One Sunday in November Fani was listening to the sermon, and the Holy Spirit spoke to her heart. This is the way she tells what happened: "That day when I accepted Christ as my personal Savior was the most precious day of my life. I understood that Jesus forgave me and He could enter my life. I was joyful and I felt so different—like a new person. When I went home, I immediately told my mother that I was a new person.

Since that day I have understood the significance of the cross and of Jesus' precious blood. My life now has meaning."

Fani was saved in 1985 and has been growing up in her salvation. Now she not only wears her gold cross, but she understands the importance of Jesus' death on the cross. When she reads about blood in the Bible, she is no longer confused, but deeply grateful for Jesus' sacrifice for her. Her sister Vicki has also come to know Jesus!

The Runaway

For over a week, young Pham Van Nam had gone to listen to the missionaries in his village tell about a man called Jesus.

"Is there anyone here who would like to ask Jesus Christ into his heart?" the missionaries asked one night. Pham's hand shot up almost before he could think.

"All those who raised their hands, please come up, and we will pray with you," the missionaries continued.

That night, Pham asked Jesus into his heart. It was just an ordinary night. No bells went off. No rockets flashed. No fireworks lit the sky. But Pham's heart changed.

Pham and his family lived in the Mekong Delta of Vietnam. His father, a businessman, served on the district court. And everyone *knew* Pham would grow up to be just like his father. The night he asked Jesus into his heart, Pham could hardly wait to tell his father the good news. Running all the way home, he burst through the door shouting, "Father! Father!"

"What is it, son?" his father asked, afraid something bad had happened.

"I asked Jesus Christ into my heart tonight!"

For the next four years, Pham went to church, studied the Bible and grew strong in the Lord. But one day, something strange happened to Pham. He was kneeling in his room, praying as he always did. Suddenly a strange idea popped into his mind: You should become a minister and preach the gospel so that people will know about Jesus. Puzzled, Pham stopped praying. *What kind of a thought was that? Was it from God?* he wondered.

"Who me, Lord?" Pham said. "I must be dreaming. You can't be putting the idea of being a minister in *my* mind?"

Even though he did not want to believe it, the idea of being a minister stuck with Pham. "Go and preach. Go and preach." The words rattled around inside his head for weeks.

"God, I can't preach," he said one night. "Send my brother. He's a good student. He's a good speaker. In fact, he's an all-around good guy, Lord. Send Him!"

Do you remember what man in the Bible said the same thing when God called him to rescue the people of Israel from the Egyptians? "I can't do this!" Moses told God over and over. At last, in desperation, Moses said, "O Lord, please send someone else to do it."

I'm not smart enough. It won't work. What if? Sometimes we all feel as if we can't do what God wants us to do. And that's exactly how Pham felt.

His head ached from trying to figure a way out of this problem. Sure, God needed people to preach, but it just couldn't be that God wanted him.

Finally, Pham couldn't deny it anymore. "All right, Lord," he said. "I'll be whatever you want me to be." So when Pham grew up, he went to Bible school in Danang. There, he met a Christian woman and got married. Together, he and his wife worked for the Lord in places all over South Vietnam. First, they worked in the Mekong Delta, then in Danang, then among the Koho tribe of mountain people near Dalat. Then they taught for 10 years at the Biblical and Theological Institute in Nhatrang.

For years, Pham and his wife worked to help people know the Lord. Lots of exciting things happened to them during this time, but the most exciting thing happened when they had to leave their country of South Vietnam because of a war.

Because of the fighting, Pham's family was in danger. One of his sons, Pham Quang Khiem, was a pilot for the South Vietnamese Air Force. He had worked out a plan to get his family safely out of the country. When the time arrived, he rushed home and told them to get ready to leave. "Meet me in one hour at the Long Thanh airport. I'll have a plane ready to fly us out of Vietnam."

Rev. Nam gathered all 56 people together. They packed only what they could carry and headed for the airport.

In the meantime, Pham Quang took a C-130 transport plane from his air base. He and another pilot were assigned to fly a special mission but decided to disobey orders and take the plane. They landed at the airfield just as Pham's family arrived.

"Hurry! Get into the plane!" Pham Quang shouted.

"Here come some soldiers!" the other pilot cried out. "Let's get out of here!"

The C-130 taxied down the runway, gathering speed. They turned to take off just as the soldiers pulled alongside. They pointed their guns at the plane, motioning them to stop. Pham Quang thought they would not shoot and ignored their demands. Soon the plane was in the air.

"Whew!" everyone sighed. "That was close!"

"Where will we go?" Rev. Nam asked his son.

"To Singapore, Father. We'll be safe there until we can figure out a way to get to the United States."

The plane with Rev. Nam's family made its way to Singapore. When they arrived in Singapore, the government didn't know what to do with them.

"You can't stay here," they said. "Go somewhere else!"

"We can't," Pham Quang told them. "We don't have any more fuel, and we don't have the money to buy any."

At last the government decided the family could stay. They were put into the local jail for a while, but as soon as the war was over, they were released and treated as heroes. Then their dreams came true. They flew to the United States to begin a whole new life.

Rev. Nam did not just sit back and relax when he got to America. He continued working hard, teaching Vietnamese people who have escaped to America.

"Who me, Lord?" Pham Nam had once asked. But after 50 years, he does not ask that anymore.

For additional copies of *Bare, Beautiful Feet and Other Missionary Stories for Children* or other titles in this series, contact your local Christian bookstore or call Christian Publications toll-free 1-800-233-4443.

Titles available:

Bare, Beautiful Feet and Other Missionary Stories for Children

A Happy Day for Ramona and Other Missionary Stories for Children

The Pink and Green Church and Other Missionary Stories for Children

The Potato Story and Other Missionary Stories for Children